Oxford University Press, Walton Street, Oxford OX2 6DP
Oxford   New York   Toronto
Delhi   Bombay   Calcutta   Madras   Karachi
Petaling Jaya   Singapore   Hong Kong   Tokyo
Nairobi   Dar es Salaam   Cape Town
Melbourne   Auckland

and associated companies in
Berlin   Ibadan

Oxford is a trade mark of Oxford University Press

Text © Lynn Zirkel 1989
Illustration © Peter Bowman 1989

British Library Cataloguing in Publication Data
Zirkel, Lynn
The shell dragon.
I. Title   II. Bowman, Pete
823'.914[J]   PZ7
ISBN 0-19-279838-3

Printed in Singapore

The Shell Dragon

Written by Lynn Zirkel

Illustrated by Peter Bowman

Oxford University Press

Oxford   New York   Toronto

A long long, time ago

sea shells were rare and precious things.

Everyone told stories about them and the one place in the world where they were washed up on the beach.

That one place was far away. A beautiful cove where the bright shells that covered the sand glowed with all the colours of the sea.

SET in the cliffs that surrounded the cove was a deep cavern. Every day the sun shone down and reflected the light from the mother of pearl that decorated its walls.

The cavern was the home of the shell dragon. The dragon had lived amongst the shells for as long as she could remember and thought of them as her own treasure.

EVERY morning and evening great, fierce, white fishing birds would fly in with the tides, bringing fish for the shell dragon to eat. The birds would always rest for a while on the dragon's tail and pass the time of day.

ONE morning, when the
big white birds had returned
to the sea, a small land bird
with a golden beak flew into
the cove. The bird had flown
many miles over the sea in
search of a warmer winter
home.

HE had a merry song to sing of his travels, which cheered the dragon who was often lonely. In return for his news she gave the bird a small silver shell.

Aꜰᴛᴇʀ a while the small bird flew away, leaving the
cove and his new friend far behind. As he flew, the sun
caught the silver shell in its golden eye. Like a tiny jewel it
glistened and shone, attracting the attention of a group of
men working in the fields below. Excited by the dazzling
shell, the men shouted and waved. The small bird was
startled by their loud noise. He was afraid of the men and
turned back towards the safety of the cove and his only
friend in this new and strange land.

FLYING fast, he soon became tired and stopped to rest in the leafy green of an old oak tree. It was then he noticed that the men were following him, for he saw their reflection in the silver shell as clearly as if it were a mirror.

Evening hung in the sky like dust as the small bird arrived back at the cove.

'Men are coming,' the small bird sang in a warning song, 'lots of men.'

THE shell dragon lifted her great head over the height of the sheltering cliffs and looked inland. She too was afraid of men. Were they coming to take her shells away? She did not know their ways, and so she called the big white fishing birds around her and waited.

As the men reached the cliffs and looked down on the cove, they were stunned by the beauty that greeted them. The size of the dragon as blue as the ocean. The birds as white as the white horses that rode on the waves . . . and the shells. Just the very sight of the shells would have fulfilled all their dreams and filled them with stories to tell.

BUT the fierce white
fishing birds were restless
and, sensing the fear of the
dragon, they attacked.

THEY dived at the men who cried out in anger at the warning touch of sharp beaks.

A great fight broke out. Shells were crushed and feathers flew, billowing like clouds tinted pink in the setting of the sun. They swirled and danced in the breeze from the sea, and one very small feather floated down on to the ticklish tip of the dragon's nose.

THE dragon could feel the start of a sneeze. It began with a hint of a tickle and swelled and swelled to a stormy size.

She tried very hard to hold it inside, for a dragon's sneeze is very destructive, but though she was big and strong the giant sneeze escaped with a thunderous roar.

It raced round the cove like a mighty whirlwind, gathering speed and collecting everything up in its path.

IT lifted the fierce white fishing birds up high to skies they had never flown. It lifted the massive weight of the dragon.

IT took her and spun her far away to a place out at sea where ships never sail and fish never swim. It is said that where she landed there sits a rock as bright and as blue as the sea that surrounds it.

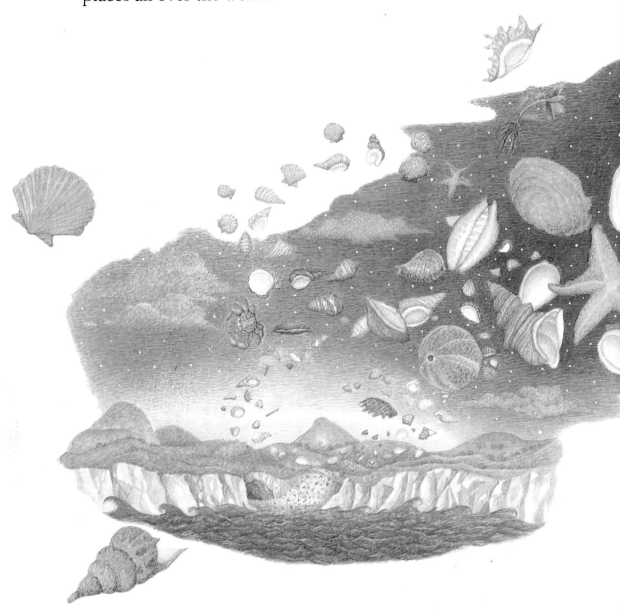

THE shells too were lifted high in a rainbow spiral of tumbling colours, and as the winds that carried them dropped to gentle breezes they were set down in lots of places all over the world.

SEA shells are now an everyday treasure and that is a
good thing. Everyone loves to collect them and make
things out of them, or sometimes just lift them and listen
for the faraway sounds of the sea.